Curious George®

Car Wash

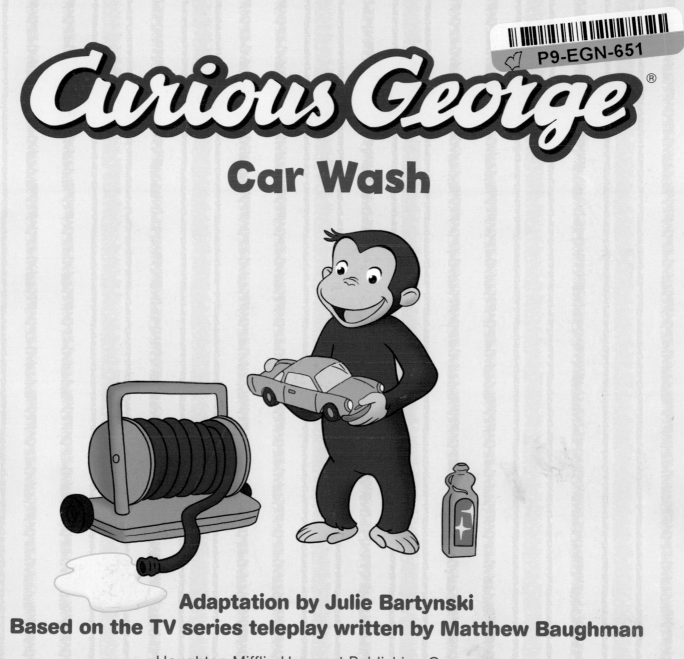

Adaptation by Julie Bartynski
Based on the TV series teleplay written by Matthew Baughman

Houghton Mifflin Harcourt Publishing Company
Boston   New York   2013

For information about permission to reproduce selections from this book, write to Permissions, Houghton Mifflin Harcourt Publishing Company, 215 Park Avenue South, New York, New York 10003.

ISBN: 978-0-544-03251-4 paper-over-board
ISBN: 978-0-547-94086-1 paperback
Design by Afsoon Razavi
www.hmhbooks.com
Printed in China
LEO 10 9 8 7 6 5 4 3 2 1
4500400009

On Saturdays, George liked to help wash the car. Sometimes his friend Allie helped too. But today the man with the yellow hat had a surprise for them. "Instead of washing the car ourselves, why don't we take it to a car wash?" the man asked.

They drove to the new automated car wash in town.

"Welcome! We do it all here—rinse, wipe, suds, scrubbers, final rinse, and towel dry at the finish line," said the car wash attendant.
The man with the yellow hat paid the attendant and they drove through the entrance.

Once inside, George noticed something strange. The man had turned off the car, but it was still moving. "The rails have rollers on them that carry our car through the wash," said the man. "It's called a conveyor belt."

First the car went through the initial rinse that made a spish spish sound.

Next came the flaps that wiped against the car. Flap! Flap!

Then George and Allie heard the blub blub of the soapsuds.

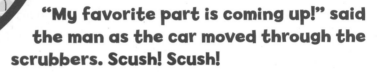

"My favorite part is coming up!" said the man as the car moved through the scrubbers. Scush! Scush!

After the scrubbers came the spish spish of the final rinse before the exit.

"That was fun! I wish we could do it again," Allie said when they got back to the house. Then George realized—he had a water sprayer, soap, and even some cars. They could build their own automated toy car wash!

First they needed a building to drive through. They decided to use two picnic table benches. When pushed together, the benches made an entrance and an exit, with plenty of car-washing space in the middle.

Next they had to create the spish spish of the rinse. But the water was too strong when sprayed directly out of the hose.

George had an idea. He needed something that would let the water out, but not all at once. He found a strainer in the kitchen. Now the car got wet but wouldn't be knocked over by the water.

"We need something to wipe the car off and make the flap flap noise," said Allie. What could they use that made the same sound? A mop! George found one inside and set it between the benches.

With the mop in place, George poured the soap on the car, but there were no bubbles. He needed something with holes that would help make the blub blub of the soap suds.

In the cupboard he found a tea strainer. He took it outside and filled it with soap and Allie sprayed water into it. They created perfect soapsuds for their car wash!

Next the scrubbers had to be added. Luckily, George found everything he needed in the bathroom.

"How do we make them scrub?" asked Allie.

George was curious. How could they get the brushes to move?

He noticed that when Allie walked forward with the sprayer, the hose spun around in its holder. That was it! George would use the hose spinner to move the scrubbers.

But something was still missing.
Of course! George remembered
the rails and rollers that carried
their car through the car wash.
He found some paint rollers, but when
he tried to add the rails, they rolled off.

"We need one of those long black mats that move, like the one at the grocery store," said Allie.
George didn't have a long black mat, but he did have short blue ones.

With the mats in place, they were ready to try out their toy car wash!

The car moved through the spish spish of the first rinse and the flap flap of the mop.

Next came the blub blub soapsuds and the scush scush scrubbers.

Another spish spish for the final rinse, and the toy car was ready for a quick towel dry. It worked!

Now George and Allie had only one thing left to do—open for business!

Soapy Sounds

Curious George and Allie loved the sounds they heard inside the automated car wash. Try matching the sounds below with the pictures of the coordinating car wash part.

1. FLAP FLAP

Rinse

2. SPISH SPISH

Wipe

3. SCUSH SCUSH

Suds

4. BLUB BLUB

Scrubbers

Sounds of Home

Machines can make all different noises. Walk around your home and listen. What sounds do you hear? What machines are making the sounds? Write down the sounds and machines on a piece of paper. Using your list, test a family member or friend to see if they can identify the machine by the sound it makes.

The Stages of a Car Wash

George and Allie had to remember the different stages they went through in the automated car wash in order to create their own toy car wash. They used everyday household items for each of the different steps, and made sure to put them in the right order.

Look at the images below. Each picture shows a different stage in George and Allie's toy car wash. Can you guess the correct order? Here's a hint: one of these items gets used twice!

SCRUBBERS

WIPE

TOWEL DRY

SUDS

RINSE

Answer key: rinse, wipe, suds, scrubbers, rinse, towel dry